Your words are worthy.
Your voice is important.

PUBLISH HER JOURNALS VI-XIV

© Copyright 2023 Publish Her Press

ISBN: 978-1-962457-03-3 (Storyteller)
ISBN: 978-1-962457-04-0 (Write On)
ISBN: 978-1-962457-05-7 (Let's Fucking Go)
ISBN: 978-1-962457-06-4 (I Bring Books to the Bar)
ISBN: 78-1-962457-07-1 (I'd Rather Be Writing)
ISBN: 978-1-962457-08-8 (Slaying the Day)
ISBN: 978-1-962457-09-5 (Shitty First Draft)
ISBN: 978-1-962457-20-0 (Overthrowing the Patriarchy)
ISBN: 978-1-962457-21-7 (Doing My Best)

Printed in the United States of America
First Printing: 2023

Published by Publish Her, LLC
310 1/2 Main Street South
Stillwater, Minnesota 55082
www.publishherpress.com

Publish Her is a female-founded publisher dedicated to elevating the words, stories and writing of women.

www.ingramcontent.com/pod-product-compliance
Lightning Source LLC
Chambersburg PA
CBHW070319010526
44107CB00004B/356